OFF-ROADING VEHICLES

DUNE BUGGIES

TAMRA B. ORR

Mitchell Lane
PUBLISHERS

Parent and Caregiver Tips for Creating Nonfiction Readers

The high-interest topics in the *Off-Roading Vehicles* series are sure to get your young reader excited about reading nonfiction. While exploring a fascinating subject, your reader will be introduced to new concepts, facts, ideas, and vocabulary.

Tips for Reading Nonfiction

Talk about Nonfiction

Explain that nonfiction books provide facts about real-world topics. When readers read nonfiction, they gain a rich understanding of the world. They build background knowledge that provides a foundation for learning and academic success.

Look at the Parts

This book contains the following helpful features. Share the purpose of each feature with your reader.

Photos, Captions, and Graphic Aids
The photos, captions, charts, maps, and other graphic aids in nonfiction texts contain a wealth of information. Help your reader identify different ways information can be displayed. A special feature, "A Closer Look," puts the spotlight on learning through images.

Sidebars
These extra tidbits of information help satisfy readers' curiosity and expand their knowledge.

Table of Contents
Located at the front of the book, this list shows the big ideas within the text and the page numbers where they can be found.

Glossary
Located at the back of the book, the glossary defines key words and phrases that are related to the topic. These words and phrases can be found in the text in **bold** type.

Comprehension Questions (Fact Check)
Multiple-choice questions help readers self-check to make sure they understand what they read.

Index
Located at the back of the book, the index is an alphabetical list of topics and the page numbers where they can be found.

With a little help and guidance, your reader will be on their way to enjoying and learning from nonfiction books.

Mitchell Lane
PUBLISHERS
mitchelllanepub.com

2001 SW 31st Avenue
Hallandale, FL 33009

First Edition, 2026.
Author: Tamra B. Orr
Designer: Kathy Walsh
Editor: Tricia Hoffman

Series: Off-Roading Vehicles
Title: Dune Buggies / by Tamra B. Orr

Hallandale, FL : Mitchell Lane Publishers, [2026]

Library bound ISBN: 979-8-89260-565-6
Paperback ISBN: 979-8-89260-595-3
eBook ISBN: 979-8-89260-572-4

Photo Credits
Adobe: background, miloje; Alamy: p22 & 29, ZarkePix; p 13 & 28; p 24 & 29, Jim West; p 10, Cephas Picture Library Ltd; p 13, steve bly; p14, Matthew Richardson; p16, Patti McConville; p17, Keystone Press; p24, Jim West; NASA @Wiki; Dreamstine: p6, Elder Salles; p 12, Ivan Mikhaylov; Shutterstock: p 15 & 28, Art Konovalov, p 21 & 29, Satheesh_ Madh; p9 & 28, betto rodriques; Cover & Title pg, Shadow of light; p4, Leo Moitinho; p 8, sylv1rob1; p18, Maciej Kopaniecki; p19, NicholasGeraldinePhotos; p20, pixinoo; p23, FOTOADICTA; p27, Longlon

Contents

Let's Go to the Beach!

Sunscreen? √ Check

Sun hat? √ Check

Sunglasses? √ Check

You are ready to go to the beach. But this time, you aren't going to swim or play in the sand.

Instead, you're climbing behind the wheel of a dune buggy. So, get ready for an off-roading adventure!

Climb On!

Dune buggies are off-roading vehicles designed for sandy, uneven **terrain**. They are made to go over sand dunes, across beaches, or through deserts.

Dune buggies have large, wide tires and open bodies. That means these vehicles have no roof, doors, or windows! The driver and rider have clear views of their surroundings, while the vehicle stays lightweight and easy to **maneuver**.

The First Dune Buggies

The first dune buggy was built in the early 1960s. It was called the Sportster. Although it was made to explore beaches, it was made of metal. This made it heavy and clunky—and not great on the sand.

A short time later, surfer, engineer, and boat builder Bruce Meyers built his own version of a dune buggy. He made it out of **fiberglass** instead of metal. As a boat builder, he was familiar with fiberglass. This made the vehicle much lighter. He named it the Meyers Manx.

The Meyers Manx had rounded headlights and was built on the lightweight frame of a Volkswagen Beetle. Meyers shortened the VW's frame by about 14 inches (36 cm).

CHECK FOR THE CAT

All original Manx buggies have a special logo—a Manx cat with a short, stubby tail. It was only put on about 6,000 models.

GAS

The World Takes Notice

In 1967, Bruce Meyers entered the Baja 1000. This is an intense endurance race over rough terrain held in Mexico each year. He won! The world took notice of the Meyers Manx.

FIT FOR A SUPERHERO

For more than 50 years, dune buggies have been featured in movies, television shows, and comic books. In 2015, a special dune buggy model was built for Spiderman. The Spidermobile came equipped with web-shooters and an ejector seat.

After his victory, Meyers' dune buggy was featured on the cover of *Car and Driver* magazine. "Once that article hit, we had 350 orders almost overnight," said Meyers.

Soon, people began stripping down Volkswagen Beetles to their frames or **chassis**. Then, they modified them into dune buggies. Many of them bought custom building kits to complete their new off-road vehicles.

By the 1970s, dune buggies were appearing more and more on beaches. With their wide tires and light, open bodies, they raced across the sand. But they did not go on streets.

ON THE MOON

The dune buggy's design inspired the creation of NASA's lunar rover. It's sometimes called the Moon buggy—rhyming with dune buggy! It was used during several Apollo missions.

Today's Buggies

Amazingly, more than 50 years after showing off the Manx, the Meyers brand is still producing dune buggies. They also sell kits to people who want to build their own models.

In 2022, the company unveiled its latest model—an all-electric version of their famous dune buggy, the Meyers Manx 2.0 EV. It can reach speeds of up to 25 miles (40.2 km) per hour. It has a 300-mile (482.8-km) battery range. This model costs approximately $74,000!

Although Meyers died in 2021, his company's new owner, Phillip Sarofim, says their new models are designed "to carry his [Meyers'] **legacy** into the future."

In 1967, *Car and Driver* described the Meyers Manx as "more soul-freeing, leaping, bounding, uninhibited fun than anything else they've ever driven—on or off the road." That is a great legacy to keep going.

Bruce Meyers

Play it Safe!

First thing's first—wearing the right safety equipment is essential for drivers and passengers, especially since most of these off-road vehicles do not have seat belts! While most models do include a **roll bar** to protect riders if the vehicle rolls over, that is not enough protection.

All riders need a safety-certified helmet. You also need goggles to protect your eyes from wind, sand, and bright sunshine.

R4

Putting on the right clothes when racing along the beach or climbing a sand dune is also important. Your usual beachwear of shorts or swimsuits may put you at risk in an emergency.

Experts recommend dune buggy riders wear long-sleeved shirts and pants. They also suggest full-finger gloves for a better grip on the steering wheel, and closed-toed boots.

EARNING SCREEN TIME

The *Fast and Furious* **franchise** featured a dune buggy race in their animated show, "Spy Racers." In 2022's *Watch Out, We're Mad*, a dune buggy is the focus of the whole film.

On- and Off-Road Adventuring

Dune buggies were designed to be driven across sand, but several types of buggies have been adapted for different terrain.

Sand rails are a type of dune buggy made especially for riding and jumping on sand dunes. Their frames are made with welded steel tubes, and they have smooth front tires. Other buggies are modified to ride on mud and snow. Some can handle rocky terrain and steep inclines.

Dune buggies need many **modifications** in order to be driven on streets. Owners need to add windshield wipers, headlights, seat belts, turn signals, different brakes, multiple mirrors, a **speedometer**, and license plates.

IN THE TREES

Some dune buggies are modified into "wood buggies." They're built to go into the forest, between trees, and over hills. They have side bars to protect riders from low branches.

Time to Race

Racing a dune buggy is quite the adventure. Races are held all over the world. If there's sand, then chances are, there may be a race there!

Some races take days to complete. The Mint 400, known as "The Great American Off-Road Race™," is held in Nevada. The 400-mile (643.7-km) course draws the world's top drivers.

The NORRA Mexican 1000 begins in Mexico. Riders travel 1,000 miles (1,609.3 km) over six days.

UP FOR THE CHALLENGE?

Thousands of racers have attempted the challenging course of the Mint 400—but fewer than half of those racers finished!

Ride the Waves ... of Sand!

Spending time on the sand is always fun, especially in a dune buggy. For more than 60 years, people have been buying or building their own models to ride on the beach and over sand dunes.

Some riders have described being in a dune buggy as riding waves of sand. Whether you're climbing in for a fun experience, saving up to buy a kit to make one, or entering a national race, fun is almost guaranteed!

LICENSE REQUIRED

Dune buggies are like cars—most states require that you are at least 16 years old and have a driver's license to get behind the wheel.

A Closer Look

Are the original Meyers Manx still around today?

Yes! You may be able to see one of these original vehicles at a classic car show in your area. But remember, only about 6,000 Meyers Manx were made. The rest are considered look-alikes!

When did the lunar rover drive on the moon?

The lunar rover was used on missions to the moon in the 1970s. The lunar rover had titanium cleats and its wheels were made out of piano wire. This gave it good traction on the moon's surface.

Will electric dune buggies become more popular?

Probably! Electric dune buggies are still being explored and developed. They will likely have more power and speed than in the past.

Why is this dune buggy kicking up so much sand?

This driver is speeding through sand dunes in Qatar, which kicks up the sand behind him. He is doing a technique called side slope.

Can dune buggies be driven on streets?

No, not without modifying them. To drive a dune buggy legally on the street, you may need to add headlights, seat belts, turn signals, license plates, and more. Check the laws in your state to make sure you're meeting the requirements.

Where are these dune buggies racing?

They're racing at the Mint 400, which is held just outside Las Vegas, Nevada. It consists of a 100-mile (160.9-km) loop that must be completed four times! It's the oldest off-road race in the U.S. and is held in March every year.

Glossary

chassis (CHAS-ee)
the frame of a vehicle, on which the body is assembled

fiberglass (FYE-bur-glas)
a strong material made from very fine glass fibers

franchise (FRAN-chize)
a set of creative works and related merchandise that share a fictional world, i.e. movies, TV shows, books, or games

legacy (LEG-uh-see)
anything handed down from one generation to another

maneuver (muh-NOO-vur)
to move something carefully

modifications (mah-duh-fi-KAY-shuhnz)
a change or adjustment

roll bar (rohl bahr)
a heavy steel bar that provides safety to passengers in the event of a roll over

speedometer (spi-DAH-mi-tur)
an instrument on a vehicle that tells you how fast you are traveling

terrain (tuh-RAYN)
a section of land

Fact Check

1. Most dune buggies come equipped with a _____.
   A. headlights B. seat belt C. roll bar
2. The Meyers Manx 2.0 is _____.
   A. for racing B. only $500 C. all-electric
3. The Mint 400 is held in ______.
   A. Florida B. Nevada C. Mexico
4. The dune buggy model was an inspiration for the design of _____.
   A. VW Beetles B. NASA's lunar rover C. race cars

Answers: 1. C, 2. C, 3. B, 4. B

Further Reading

Abdo, Kenny. *Dune Buggies (Off Road Vehicles)*. ABDO Publishing, 2017.

Hale, James. *The Dune Buggy Handbook: The A-Z of VW-Based Buggies Since 1964*. Veloce Publishing Ltd., 2017

Marks, Jennifer. *Dune Buggies*. Blazers, 2006.

Tieck, Sarah. *Dune Buggies (Amazing Vehicles)*. Buddy Books/National Science Foundation, 2009.

On the Internet

Dune Buggies: Everything You Need to Know
sand-boarding.com/dune-buggy/
Learn more about the history of dune buggies and the different types available today.

How Dune Buggies Work
www.mapquest.com/travel/outdoor-activities/off-roading/dune-buggies.htm
Explore the differences between sand rails, swamp buggies, and dune buggies.

Manx 2.0 EV
meyersmanx.com/pages/2-0-ev
Watch the all-electric Meyers Manx 2.0 being tested on the beach in Baja, California.

Index

About the Author

Tamra B. Orr is a mom, wife, grandmother, and full-time writer and author living in the beautiful all-terrain Pacific Northwest. She lives in a state with more than 350 miles of coastline for dune buggy drivers to explore. The Oregon Dunes National Recreation Area has some of the largest dunes in the country. A graduate of Ball State University, she has written more than 750 nonfiction and educational books for readers of all ages and loves her job. It gives her the chance to learn about something new—and then share that information with readers of all ages—every single day.